Plains Indians

CONTENTS

© Aladdin Books Ltd

Designed and produced by
Aladdin Books Ltd
70 Old Compton Street
London W1

First published in the
United States in 1984 by
Gloucester Press
387 Park Avenue South
New York NY 10016

ISBN 0-531-03479-8

Library of Congress
Catalog Card No. 77-12087

*Certain illustrations have previously appeared in the "CivilizationLibrary"
series published by Gloucester Press*

THE CIVILIZATION LIBRARY

Plains Indians

JILL HUGHES

Illustrated by
MAURICE WILSON
GEORGE THOMSON

Consultant
NORMAN BANCROFT-HUNT

Gloucester Press
New York · Toronto · 1984

People of the Great Plains

In the middle of North America there is a huge area of flat, grass-covered land. This land is known as the Great Plains. About three hundred years ago, the only people who lived here were the American Indians.

They were given the name "Indians" because the first white people to discover America thought they had found a new way to India. But the Indians had their own names for themselves, such as Pawnee, Blackfoot, and Sioux for example. They lived in different tribes, or nations, and each of these spoke its own language. Some of the Plains Indians were hunters who moved from place to place and lived all year in tents, called tepees. Others lived in villages, and spent some of their time farming, but they too used tepees when they went hunting.

Sioux

Pawnee

Kansa

Blackfoot

4

A hard homeland

Life on the Plains was hard; in summer it was hot and dry, in winter there were freezing winds and deep snow. Even during the warm spring there could be a sudden unexpected storm that might freeze a man or animal to death. But as long as the Indians were able to hunt the buffalo, they could be sure of meat to eat and warm skins to make clothes and tepees. When the white people began to move onto the Great Plains, thoughtlessly killing the buffalo with their guns, the old hunting life of the Indians started to come to an end.

The Great Plains

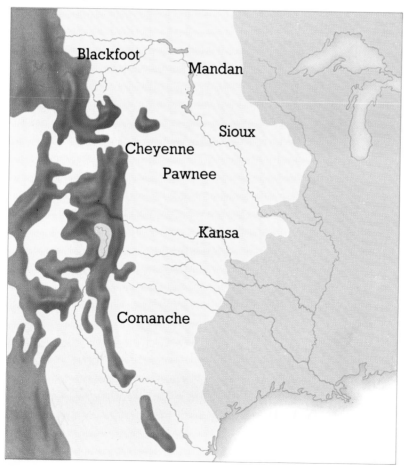

The map shows where the different tribes lived on the Plains. The yellow areas are short grass, the pale green areas are long grass and the dark green patches, mountains.

5

Hunting the buffalo

Most of the buffalo spent the winter far to the south. Then, when spring arrived, they began to move north in search of good places to graze, and to reach their breeding grounds by the summer. Sometimes there were so many buffalo, stretching over the Plains as far as the eye could see, that the land looked black.

This was an exciting time for the Indians. The tribe, which had split up into small bands for the winter, gathered together and old friends met again. Many dances and feasts were held. But most important, everyone joined together for the big summer hunts.

Great skill was needed to shoot a charging buffalo, while moving at high speed on horseback.

Hunting skills

The Indians hunted on horseback. Their ponies were specially chosen and trained to run fast and turn quickly. A hunter's life depended on his pony's skill in avoiding a buffalo if it turned and charged. The buffalo is a big heavy animal, and can be very dangerous. It is important to kill it cleanly and quickly. The Indians used bows and arrows, or spears, and aimed to hit the buffalo behind the shoulder blades, where the arrow or spear would reach the heart. The bows used for hunting buffalos were prized possessions and very powerful. It was not unusual for an arrow to pass right through a buffalo!

Hunting the buffalo

Before they had horses, the Indians hunted on foot, disguised in wolf skins.

A buffalo herd could be driven into a trap by setting fire to the grass behind it.

Sometimes the herd was driven over a cliff. The dead animals were collected at the bottom.

The buffalo's gifts

After a successful hunt, the Indians said that their camps were "red with meat." The women boiled, or roasted, the meat over camp fires, and big feasts were held. Much of the meat was cut into thin strips, and smoked over the fire, or dried in the sun. This dried meat could be eaten throughout the winter. Piles of buffalo skins had to be cleaned, dried, and softened.

Using the buffalo

The cleaned skins were made into clothes, shoes (moccasins), and storage bags (parfleches). Several buffalo skins had to be sewn together to make a new cover for a tepee. Every part of the buffalo was used for something. Hooves were carved into bowls and spoons, hair twisted into rope, and the fat melted down for soap. The children even made the ribs into sledges to race down the grassy hill slopes!

Fastening buffalo skins to the ground to dry.

Coats, leggings, shoes, and robes (a kind of cloak) were all made from buffalo skin.

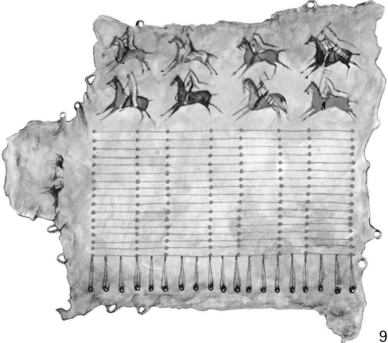

Part of the robe of a Cheyenne Indian, made of buffalo skin painted with picture writing.

The "Mystery Dog"

Indians lived on the Great Plains for thousands of years, but it was not until three hundred years ago that they got horses. The native horses of America had become extinct in prehistoric times, and the first horses the Indians used came from herds taken to the New World by Spanish explorers.

The only domestic animals the Indians had known until then were dogs. The horses altered their way of life by allowing them to travel much greater distances.

Tribes which had been farmers, living in villages, sometimes gave up their settled homes to follow the buffalo. The Indians called the horses "Mystery Dogs" because they thought there was something special and wonderful about them.

Horse riches

The Indians understood the ways of animals very well, and soon mastered horses. Sometimes tribes captured the wild horses by lassoing them with ropes of buffalo hair. The Indians could ride without saddles, and felt themselves to be part of the horse. It was said of the Comanche Indians that they rode better than they walked. To own horses soon came to be very important, especially owning those that had been trained for use in hunting and warfare.

The more well-trained horses a man had, the richer he was and the more generously he could loan them to others. The most generous men were highly respected and often became chiefs.

Because horses were worth a lot of money, they were traded (or swapped) for other valuable goods, including guns, knives, and clothes.

Other kinds of food

Besides the buffalo, other animals and plants on the Plains provided the Indians with food. All kinds of berries grew in the river valleys. Some of them could be dried and kept for winter, when they would be cooked with the dried buffalo meat to make stews. There were also many different vegetables and fruits that grew wild in great quantities on parts of the Plains. Grapes and wild onions were just some of the foods that they gathered.

In the winter especially, animals like deer and rabbits were hunted. Their furs were as valuable as their meat. Hunters often smeared their faces and hands with bear's grease to keep out the icy winds, and to hide their scent from the animals they hunted. Many tribes shot birds, and a few also caught fish.

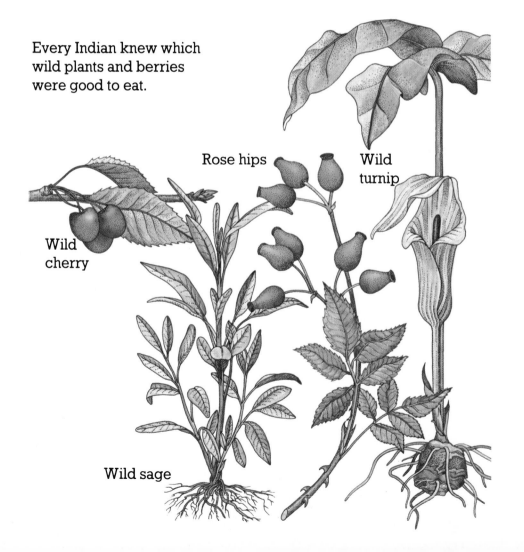

Every Indian knew which wild plants and berries were good to eat.

Rose hips

Wild turnip

Wild cherry

Wild sage

Trapping and trading

In winter the animals of the American plains and woods grow thicker coats to keep out the cold. The Indian hunters tracked them through the snow on snow shoes or shot them as they skidded on the ice of frozen rivers. The fresh meat made a welcome change from the dried stores, and the thick furs could be used for winter bedding, robes, mittens and fur caps.

They traded some of the glossy beaver or bear furs with the village Indians for their farm produce. The village tribes grew corn, beans, and pumpkins, and stored food for the winter in pits dug in the ground. They also traded with white people, exchanging furs for blankets, guns, ammunition, flour, sugar, and tobacco.

Indian village women preparing food.

It was one of the women's jobs
to put up the tepees.

Indian homes

The hunting tribes lived in tepees all the time; the village tribes used them only when on hunting expeditions. They could be put up, or taken down, quickly, and were very easy to carry around. All tepees were made of buffalo skins stretched over frameworks of tall poles. This made them very cool in summer, warm and weather-proof in winter.

A circular camp of white tepees on the green plain must have been a breathtaking sight. Sometimes the outsides of the tepees were beautifully painted and decorated, often with figures of animals' spirits which protected the tepee's owner.

The village tribes lived in houses called earth lodges. Earth and grass were piled up over wooden posts and willow branches to make houses big enough to hold forty people – and their horses and dogs!

Inside a lodge.

On the move

Before they had horses, the Plains Indians could travel only short distances in a day. They used dogs, pulling little stretchers of poles, called travois, to carry their belongings. But horses were much stronger than dogs, and could carry a lot more, over longer distances.

They could even pull old or sick people who would otherwise have been left behind. Small children were pulled on travois, too, safely tucked inside cages of basket work. Men carried only their weapons so that they could defend the tribe against attack.

A party of Blackfoot Indians on the move.

Tribal gatherings

The main advantage of being able to travel fast over long distances was to follow the buffalo herds. But tribes also traveled to meet other tribes, to trade or to join together for feasts and dances. These were very splendid occasions, when everyone wore their finest clothes, decorated with beads, fringes, and feathers. Even old enemies traded peaceably together at these big gatherings.

Although the tribes did not understand one another's speech, they could "talk" to each other in sign language. The hand signals used in sign language were understood by all Plains Indians.

Growing up

The Plains Indians believed in helping one another, and taking care of their families. They felt very close to all their relatives, and might consider someone to be a ''brother'' or ''sister'' if there was some special friendship between them, even though that person might belong to another tribe. Children were treated kindly but firmly.

They were never hit, but they were expected to grow up quickly and become useful members of the tribe. The well brought-up child carried out his parent's or grandparent's wishes without waiting to be asked, and without complaining. Even babies were taught not to cry if they wanted something. In time of war, a crying baby might tell an enemy where the tribe was hiding.

Indian children began to learn to ride early.

Different skills

Children were given names which made them part of the tribe. Often they were known to everyone by their nicknames, but they usually had a real name too. This might be an animal, or a reminder of a brave deed done by one of the tribe. Later, if a boy did something brave himself, his name could be changed.

Girls were taught by their grandmothers to cook and sew, prepare buffalo skins, and put up tepees. Boys learned to hunt. Sometimes, the boys were taken into special tents, called sweat lodges, where they were told the secrets of the animal spirits. Water was thrown on to red-hot stones in the lodge, filling it with steam.

Sweat lodges were used for bathing in, as well as for learning tribal beliefs and customs.

War and weapons

Even before white people came to America, the Indian tribes made war among themselves. But they didn't fight just to kill enemies.

They wanted to prove the bravery of their young men, and to show how well they were able to protect the tribe. To touch a live enemy, which was done with a special coup stick, snatch his weapons, and then get away without hurting him, was considered very daring. Someone who did this was looked up to in his own tribe, and respected by the warriors of other tribes.

To get extra protection in times of danger, the warrior painted himself, and usually his pony and weapons too. He sang a secret song, and carried a special charm that he had been "given" by the animal spirits who watched over him.

Coup stick

Club

Arrows in quiver

Bow in special case

Stuffed bird

Knife

Tomahawk

Magic charms, like the stuffed bird here, were carried into battle, and were as important to the warrior as his weapons.

A Blackfoot warrior in war paint and feather war bonnet.

Games and pastimes

Although life was often hard for the Plains Indians, they found time to enjoy sports and games of all kinds. Some of their games were a kind of practice for real life hunting or fighting. Little boys played at riding on stick horses (like hobby horses), before they rode on the real thing. Once they could ride, they played a rough game called "throwing-them-off-their-horses," in which they tried to wrestle each other to the ground. In the game shown in the picture below, two men try to hit a rolling hoop with poles. This often produced plenty of bruises, but was good practice for using a spear accurately when hunting, as well as being an exciting game.

Around the fire

There were quieter pastimes to be enjoyed around the camp fire. The women made skin bags and belts, which were beautifully decorated with dyed porcupine quills or beads. Their dresses and moccasins were decorated with beads too. Sometimes even the soles of the moccasins had beads on them.

While the women did their sewing and beading, the older men carved pipes for smoking, and told stories. Many of these were about the history of the tribe, but others were about the ways of nature and the animals. It was from these stories that the children learned that animals were their friends, and should not be treated cruelly or thoughtlessly. Music and dancing were both a pleasure and a way of keeping contact with the spirits of land, sky, and animals.

Mandans dancing

The Sun Dance

The Plains Indians believed that everything in the world had a soul or spirit. The most powerful spirits were those of the sun, moon and stars; of thunder and lightning; and of the birds and animals.

Because the Indians were given so many good things by the spirits, they held many ceremonies and dances, in which they sent back their thanks.

The biggest of the ceremonies was the Sun Dance, when they gave thanks for everything that had taken place in the past year, and asked the spirits to renew the world for the coming year.

Some young men felt the power of the spirits so strongly, that they could endure any pain. They fastened ropes to sharp spikes in the skin of their chests and danced, gazing at the sun, until they fainted from exhaustion.

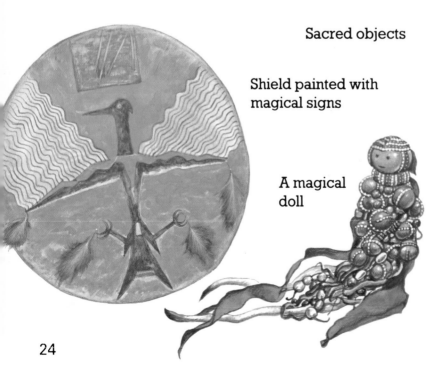

Sacred objects

Shield painted with magical signs

A magical doll

The Sun Dance

War with the white man

When Europeans first came to America, they traded with the Indians, and the Indians showed them how to live off the land. But the Europeans brought diseases with them, like measles and smallpox, that the Indians had never known. They had no resistance to the diseases and died in large numbers.

More and more white people came to America, and they needed more land. They began to build settlements in the hunting grounds of the Indians, and killed many of the buffalo on which the Indians depended. At last the warriors decided to try and stop them.

The US army had made a peace treaty with the Cheyenne Indians. In 1864 the army broke the treaty and attacked a Cheyenne camp, killing men, women, and children.

The War of the West

The government of the United States encouraged the white settlers to "open up" the country – to build houses, raise cattle, and grow crops. Sometimes the government made agreements, or treaties, with the Indians for their land, but often it just allowed the white people to take the land by force. The government built a railroad across the Plains.

The Indians called a railroad an "iron horse." When the government ignored the agreements it had made, the Indians fought back, and the government declared war.

The Indians' defeat

The bitter Plains wars between the US government and the Indians lasted for nearly forty years. It was not just land for settlers that the government wanted. Gold had been discovered in the Black Hills of Dakota.

This was the land of the Sioux. They joined together with the Cheyenne in a desperate attempt to fight off the US army. Led by chiefs Crazy Horse, and Sitting Bull, the Indians were successful at first. When the American General Custer attacked their camp, he was defeated and all his men were killed. However, after this, the army just sent more troops. The huge numbers of well-trained soldiers and their guns were too much for the Indians. By the 1870s most of them had been driven on to reservations and their weapons taken away.

Indians being marched to a reservation by the US army.

28

One last hope

The Indians had not only been defeated in battle but, with the fencing in of the Plains for farms and ranches and the killing of the buffalo, they had lost their livelihood. All over the Plains, Indians began dancing the Ghost Dance, believing that if they danced long enough, and hard enough, the whites would go, and the buffalo would return.

They wore "ghost shirts," which they thought would protect them against the settlers' bullets, because the whites would be afraid to attack them. But when three hundred Sioux, wearing ghost shirts, were shot down by the US army, they knew that the struggle to keep their old way of life was over.

Indians performing the Ghost Dance, asking the buffalo to return to their old hunting grounds.

A new world

The life of the Indians on the reservations was a sad one. Their special skills as warriors and hunters were useless, and the government banned many of the dances and ceremonies. They were prisoners on the reservations. The US government wanted the Indians to be farmers, but often the land was too poor and nothing would grow. Some of the hunters refused to dig in their sacred Mother Earth, because it was against their beliefs.

The Bureau of Indian Affairs, which was supposed to look after the Indians, made them send their children away to boarding schools where they could not learn the tribal ways and were forbidden to speak their own languages. Even reservation land was broken up and sold.

Hope for the future?

In recent years the Indians have begun to fight back again, but in a different way. Many children now go to schools on the reservations, and learn their own language and tribal history. Indian lawyers are fighting the government in the law courts according to white people's rules. With the spirits' help, and the help of the lawyers, perhaps the Plains Indians will one day live again in freedom and dignity in this white man's world.

Glossary

Coup stick A stick with special magic power used by an Indian warrior to touch an enemy.

Cradleboard A kind of bag, of skin and wood, used by Indian mothers to carry their babies.

Earth lodge A large house for many people, of earth and grass piled up over a frame of wood.

Iron horse The name the Indians gave to the railroad.

Lacrosse A ball game played by two teams with nets on sticks in which they catch the ball.

Picture writing The only written language of the Indians in which stories were told in pictures.

Reservations Lands where the Indians were kept after they had been driven from the Plains.

Sun Dance A dance held in summer to ask the spirits of the buffalo to bring good luck to the tribe.

Travois A framework of sticks, pulled by a dog or a horse, on which things could be carried.

Index

32

PRINTED IN BELGIUM BY

proost
INTERNATIONAL BOOK PRODUCTION